Professional Military Ethics Series

RESOLVING ETHICAL CHALLENGES IN AN ERA OF PERSISTENT CONFLICT

Tony Pfaff

I0447252

April 2011

*****

Comments pertaining to this report are invited and should be forwarded to: Director, Strategic Studies Institute, U.S. Army War College, 632 Wright Ave, Carlisle, PA 17013-5046.

*****

All Strategic Studies Institute (SSI) publications may be downloaded free of charge from the SSI website. Hard copies of this report may also be obtained free of charge while supplies last by placing an order on the SSI website. The SSI website address is: *www.StrategicStudiesInstitute.army.mil*.

*****

The Strategic Studies Institute publishes a monthly e-mail newsletter to update the national security community on the research of our analysts, recent and forthcoming publications, and upcoming conferences sponsored by the Institute. Each newsletter also provides a strategic commentary by one of our research analysts. If you are interested in receiving this newsletter, please subscribe on the SSI website at *www.StrategicStudiesInstitute. army.mil/newsletter/*.

FOREWORD

This monograph is the fourth in a series on the Army's Professional Military Ethic (PME) that the Chief of Staff of the Army, General George W. Casey, Jr., inaugurated in October 2009. In his series foreword, General Casey encouraged the Army to "think critically about our PME and promote dialogue at all levels as we deepen our understanding of what this time-honored source of strength means to the profession today."

In this monograph, Colonel Tony Pfaff explores the ethical challenges facing the Army in an era of persistent conflict dominated by a variety of irregular threats. Pfaff argues that these challenges arise because irregular adversaries change the character of their war from imposing one's will on the enemy to compelling the enemy to accept one's interest. While this shift may seem subtle, Pfaff argues, it suggests a number of important practical and ethical implications for our way of war. Formerly, civilians were largely separable from warfighting, meaning that our strategies of annihilation and attrition were the most effective—and ethical—paths to victory. But now, when combating irregular threats, civilians are no longer separable from warfighting. Consequently, strategies of annihilation and attrition not only undermine a successful resolution of the conflict, but they are unethical.

This last point suggests that the Army needs to adapt the PME to account for these changes and to adopt a number of policies and procedures to account for the expanded role irregular conflicts demand Soldiers play. Colonel Pfaff offers a number of practical measures the Army should take to meet this challenge.

I invite our readers to learn more about this important topic, to test their own assumptions regarding the moral challenges posed by the changing character of war, and to initiate discussions on how our organization, the U.S. Army, should respond.

DOUGLAS C. LOVELACE, JR.
Director
Strategic Studies Institute

ABOUT THE AUTHOR

TONY PFAFF is a Foreign Area Officer for the Middle East and North Africa, currently serving as the Chief of International Military Affairs for Army Central Command. Colonel Pfaff began his military career as an Infantry officer and first served as platoon leader and company executive officer in the 82nd Airborne Division, with whom he deployed to Operations DESERT SHIELD and DESERT STORM. He then served as a company commander and battalion operations officer in the 1st Armored Division, with which he deployed to Operation ABLE SENTRY in the former Yugoslav Republic of Macedonia. Colonel Pfaff has also served on the faculty at West Point and as the Senior Intelligence Officer for the Joint Staff's Iraq Intelligence Working Group. He has served twice in Iraq, once as the Deputy J2 for a Joint Special Operations Task Force, and as the Senior Military Advisor for the Civilian Police Assistance Training Program. Most recently, he served as the Defense Attaché in Kuwait. He also served as a consultant for the Independent Panel to Review Department of Defense Detention Procedures headed by former Secretary of Defense James Schlesinger and contributed to the ethics section of the Army and Marine Corps counterinsurgency field manual. Colonel Pfaff has authored a number of articles in professional and scholarly publications including, "The Ethics of Complex Contingencies," published in *The Future of the Army Profession*, 2nd Ed, Don Snider and Lloyd Matthews, eds.; "Bungee Jumping Off the Moral High-ground: The Ethics of Espionage in the Modern Age," published in *Ethics of Spying: A Reader for the Intelligence Professional*, Jan

Goldman, ed.; "The Ethics of Espionage," in the *Journal of Military Ethics*; "Toward an Ethics of Detention and Interrogation: Consent and Limits," published in *Philosophy and Public Policy Quarterly*; and "Chaos, Complexity, and the Modern Battlefield, published in *Military Review*. Colonel Pfaff has a bachelor's degree in Philosophy and Economics from Washington and Lee University, a master's degree in Philosophy from Stanford University, and a master's in National Resource Strategy from the Industrial College of the Armed Forces.

SUMMARY

Combating irregular threats has challenged the American "way of war" in a number of ways. Not only does it challenge how U.S. forces fight, it also brings into question the ethical norms they employ to govern the fighting. The resulting confusion is especially evident in the public debate over the rules of engagement used in Afghanistan. On the one hand, many are concerned that restrictions on the use of force have placed Soldiers' lives needlessly at risk. On the other, many are concerned that risking civilian casualties is not only immoral in irregular war, but undermines the war effort.

The rules of war entail balancing three competing imperatives: (1) accomplishing the mission; (2) protecting the force; and (3) minimizing harm. Determining that balance entails determining where one should accept risk. Accomplishing missions risks Soldiers and civilians; protecting the force risks mission accomplishment and civilians; and minimizing harm risks mission accomplishment and force protection. Where risk *should* be accepted depends on the ends the use of military force is intended to achieve, as well as the character of the adversary.

To understand why the ends and adversaries associated with combating irregular threats pose special challenges to ethical decisionmaking, one must first grasp the complex relationship these competing imperatives have with the amount of risk Soldiers may accept or the amount of risk to which they may assign to others. Confronting such threats emphasizes populations rather than military forces and capabilities. In doing so, it expands the ends and means of war, requiring Soldiers not only to defend the state, but to impose civil order outside the state as well. These complications fundamentally change the character of warfare, requiring Soldiers to rethink where they may incur and assign risk when balancing the ethical demands of their profession.

This point has important implications for the way U.S. forces should fight irregular adversaries, and the norms they should employ. First, it suggests that destruction of the enemy combat capability may paradoxically put true mission accomplishment at risk, especially when civilian lives are jeopardized. Second, it suggests that as the supported government develops the capacity for governance, the use of military force must itself transition from warfighting, where some collateral damage is inevitable, to law enforcement, where it is not. This monograph will offer a number of policy recommendations to accommodate these two propositions.

What should also be obvious from this introductory framework is that the identity of the military professional will have to evolve to meet the demands of the environment of irregular conflict. The good qualities of a military professional derive from the purpose and function of the profession and the environment in which it is practiced. As the function and the environment change, so must the qualities of the good professional. This monograph will thus offer policy recommendations for future Army leader employment and development.

RESOLVING ETHICAL CHALLENGES IN AN ERA OF PERSISTENT CONFLICT

ETHICS AND COMBATING IRREGULAR THREATS

It is famously observed that in war armies often re-fight their last war. This observation suggests that military capabilities rarely evolve faster than the threats to which they must respond. The same is sometimes true for the ethics intended to regulate fighting. The ethics of war has, for the most part, evolved to govern armed conflict where the warring parties attempt to impose their will on each other. As such, militaries associated with states that recognize these restrictions have developed the weapons and tactics that permit them to destroy another state's military forces while observing their own ethical standards.[1]

But the character of warfare against irregular threats[2] is different from the kind of wars that traditional just war norms were meant to regulate. Rather than facing enemies in open battle, for which the U.S. military is well-suited, U.S. forces find themselves embroiled in complex counterinsurgencies and counter-terrorist campaigns where identifying the enemy — as well as identifying the best means to defeat him — is filled with uncertainty. This practical uncertainty entails ethical uncertainty as well: it is impossible to know what the rules of the game are if one does not know what game one is playing.

At its most basic level, the rules of war entail balancing three often-competing imperatives: (1) accomplishing the mission; (2) protecting the force; and (3) minimizing harm. Determining where the balance should lie depends on where one should accept risk.

Accomplishing missions puts Soldiers and noncombatants at risk; protecting the force puts mission accomplishment and noncombatants at risk; and minimizing harm puts mission accomplishment and force protection at risk. Where risk should be assigned depends on the ends the use of military force is intended to achieve. What those ends are depends on the character of the adversary.

To understand why the ends and adversaries associated with combating irregular threats pose special challenges to ethical decisionmaking, one must first grasp the complex relationship these competing imperatives have with the amount of risk Soldiers may take or place on others. Combating irregular threats complicates that relationship because it places emphasis on populations rather than military forces and capabilities. In doing so, it expands the ends and means of war, requiring Soldiers not only to defend the state, but to impose civil order as well. These complications fundamentally change the character of warfare and require Soldiers to rethink where they may accept and place risk when balancing the ethical demands of their profession.

THE ETHICAL PROBLEM: PERMISSIONS AND RESTRICTIONS IN THE USE OF FORCE

Nothing captures the difficulties that combating irregular threats places on the military ethic better than the recent controversy surrounding the rules of engagement (ROE) employed by U.S. Soldiers in Afghanistan. While these rules correctly recognize the importance of minimizing risk to noncombatants, they often increase the risk to Soldiers and, by extension, mission accomplishment. For example, while re-

ceiving mortar fire during an overnight mission, a sergeant requested supporting artillery fire—a 155mm
howitzer illumination round—so that his unit could
better see the enemy's location. Despite the fact that
illumination rounds are not designed to inflict casualties, higher headquarters rejected the request on the
ground that it could cause collateral damage.

Later, the same sergeant reported that his unit
came under heavy small arms and rocket propelled
grenade (RPG) fire, and he requested artillery to be
fired on the enemy's position. This support was also
denied because of the proximity of Afghan civilians
to the fighting. To break contact with the enemy, the
sergeant then requested the supporting artillery unit
to fire smoke rounds to conceal their movement. Like
illumination rounds, smoke rounds are not designed
to cause casualties, though there is always a remote
possibility that the nonexplosive canister carrying the
smoke could hit someone. But while this request was
granted, the rounds were deliberately aimed one ki-
lometer off the requested position for fear of injuring
civilians. As a result, the rounds were not effective for
concealing the unit's movement.[3]

On the other hand, playing by the traditional rules
of war, rules that permit noncombatant casualties,
comes with its own risks. For example, in late 2003,
U.S. military commanders in Iraq adopted a range of
aggressive tactics intended to increase lethality and
make the cost of resistance too high for insurgents to
bear. In response to this guidance, Soldiers went into
Iraqi towns and villages kicking in doors and detain-
ing scores of fighting-age "angry young men."[4] As one
embedded *New York Times* reporter noted, while these
measures may have been absolutely necessary, they
drained "whatever good will the Sunnis had left for
the Americans."[5]

U.S. forces have seen similar reactions to collateral damage in Afghanistan. In fact, Afghan President Hamid Karzai, responding to public outcry, has repeatedly called for International Security Assistance Forces (ISAF) to curtail operations and eliminate civilian casualties altogether.[6] Despite the fact that U.S. strikes against insurgent positions are almost always proportionate and discriminate, insurgents are often able to portray their casualties as civilian casualties. Additionally, insurgents are able to exploit the fact that Coalition forces operate in a way that tolerates noncombatant casualties. Insurgents thus portray not only their own casualties, but also the civilian casualties the insurgents themselves cause, as being a result of Coalition operations. The result is civilian outrage and calls by Karzai's government to constrain U.S. operations.[7]

What these examples show is that there is an inherent tension between the imperatives of accomplishing missions, protecting the force, and minimizing harm to noncombatants that often makes finding ethically permissible courses of action difficult. Further, these examples suggest that finding such courses of action requires assessing where to accept risk; they also suggest that where one should accept risk is situation-dependent. This means that general rules meant to cover a wide range of situations will be difficult, if not impossible, to establish. Rather, ethical behavior against irregular adversaries will be somewhat ad hoc, that is, it will require individual Soldiers and their leaders to be sensitive to local conditions at the time and the particulars of their mission, their organization, and the civilians in their area of operations.

Toward the end of articulating a method for Soldiers to make ethical decisions when combating irregular threats, the next section will discuss the competing imperatives and the impact combating irregular threats has on their application. This will allow a clearer formulation of the ethical problem from which it will be possible to determine an ethical approach better suited to the demands of this kind of war.

THE PROFESSIONAL MILITARY ETHIC: BALANCING RISK

Accomplishing the Mission.

Military ethics begins with the utilitarian imperative to accomplish missions. The logic is fairly simple. If one's cause is just, one maximizes the good by achieving it. Thus, actions that lead to victory or avoid defeat are not just permissible, they are obligatory. Additionally, it is a feature of any utilitarian ethic that the greater the good, the greater the kinds of harms that may be done in its name. While the use of weapons of mass destruction (WMD) or mass killings of noncombatants would normally be ruled out, if victory—depending on what was at stake—becomes more elusive or defeat more imminent, indiscriminate acts of violence may under certain circumstances be justified.[8]

However, this permission does entail a restraint. Though utilitarian ethics do not rule out any particular kinds of acts, they do rule out acts whose outcomes result in more harm than good.[9] This restriction, referred to as proportionality, requires Soldiers to limit the use of force relative to the value of the military objective.[10] The value of the military objective is measured against its contribution to the ethical objective of war: to establish a better state of peace than the *status quo ante bellum*.[11] Thus indiscriminate acts would most often be unjustified because the harm they cause undermines the chance for a better peace.

Protecting the Force.

In tension with the requirement to accomplish the mission is the competing requirement to protect one's Soldiers.[12] While the imperative to accomplish missions obligates officers to put their Soldiers' lives at risk, a broader view of military ethics must also consider the obligations officers have to preserve their Soldiers' lives and well-being. Such measures have both utilitarian and moral aspects to their justification. From the perspective of military necessity, officers are obligated to preserve their forces so they may continue the fight. From a deontic perspective, officers are morally bound to give force to the proposition that Soldiers are human beings with their own rights to life and liberty.[13]

Minimizing Harm.

In fact, it is these rights to life and liberty that justify fighting in the first place. Most Just War theories define war in terms of some violation of a state's political sovereignty or territorial integrity.[14] But these "state rights" are not in themselves worth defending, but rather derive their value to the extent that their preservation secures the rights of citizens to life and liberty.[15] Because these rights are universal, they restrict the kind of harms Soldiers may commit. This restriction, referred to as noncombatant immunity, requires Soldiers to discriminate when applying force and prohibits intentionally targeting civilians as well as surrendered or incapacitated enemy Soldiers.[16] Because Soldiers receive training, equipment, and other resources to reduce their risk when fighting, it follows that they must accept some additional risk if it means preserving the lives of noncombatants who, by definition, have not received those resources.[17]

The Ethical Problem.

From this admittedly brief analysis, it is easy to see how difficult ethical decisionmaking for Soldiers can be. They are required to achieve a trifecta — to win wars, preserve Soldiers' lives, and minimize harm to noncombatants. Even in conventional conflicts, where combatants are easier to distinguish from noncombatants, such a trifecta can be difficult enough. But enemies like Hamas, al Qaeda, and the Taliban are not only indistinguishable from the civilian population, they deliberately operate close to densely populated areas in order to exploit any collateral damage inflicted by our forces.[18] Figure 1 depicts the multidirectionality of forces affecting ethical decisionmaking, which entails trading off between risks associated with the triple imperatives of accomplishing the mission, protecting the force, and avoiding harm to noncombatants.

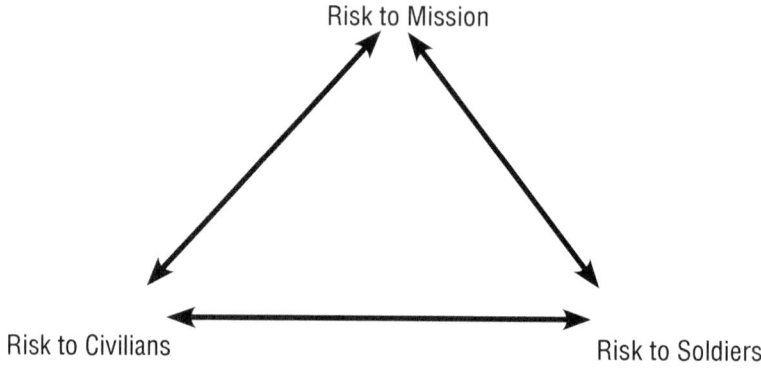

Figure 1. Ethical Decisionmaking.

This complex ethical environment places Soldiers in a difficult position. To win the war, Soldiers must find and engage the enemy within the target population, which increases their vulnerability to attack. Their alternative is to use weapons of greater lethality and range, which increases their own safety but decreases their ability to discriminate combatants from noncombatants. Further, the enemies' disregard for noncombatant lives also places enormous pressure on Soldiers to discount that constraint and thus "level the playing field." It is one thing to say the right to life is universal. It is another to say that an enemy noncombatant's right to life takes priority over the right to life of the Soldiers under an officer's charge. When the enemy intentionally places noncombatants in harm's way, they force Soldiers to weigh mission accomplishment and force protection against the rights of those noncombatants. If the risks to the mission and one's forces becomes so great as to jeopardize operational integrity, it is not clear that Soldiers are required to take those risks.[19]

What should be clear from this discussion is that the way many current adversaries fight is putting pressure on U.S. forces to change the way they fight. To explain the effects of such pressure, the next section will articulate and compare the "conventional" U.S. way of war with the irregular way of war and establish a foundation from which to articulate an ethics for combating irregular threats.

"WAYS OF WAR" AND ETHICS OF WAR

Clausewitz and the U.S. Way of War.

The Western "way of war" draws heavily on Carl von Clausewitz's view that war deals with imposing one's will on the enemy. This view entails a number of dichotomies.[20] The actors in war are either friends or enemies; actions in war entail resistance or surrender; and the end-state of war is victory or defeat. It is true that enemies may fight to a stalemate, but such a state of affairs is not stable, representing only a suspension of hostilities until the sides decide to fight again. The state of war itself continues until the hostile relationship has transformed into one of peaceful competition or one or both sides have ceased resisting the other's will.

The logic of war in the Clausewitzian view is simple in expression, but difficult in application. One has imposed one's will successfully when the enemy no longer has the capability to resist. One eliminates the enemy's capability to resist by eliminating his combat capability faster than the enemy can eliminate one's own. Doing this requires a strategy of annihilation—or at least attrition—that seeks a head-to-head battle aimed at destroying as much of the enemy's forces, as well as his ability to generate new ones, as possible.[21]

The "way of war" that emerges from this sort of confrontation with the enemy, is, as historian Victor Davis Hanson puts it, "so lethal precisely because it is so amoral — shackled rarely by concerns of ritual, tradition, religion, or ethics, by anything other than military necessity."[22] Hanson is not saying here that Western militaries do not often observe restraint in war. His point is that Western and, by extension, American thinking on war is driven by the idea of "enemy as existential threat" who must be defeated in order to preserve the kinds of individual freedoms that have shaped western societies since the time of the ancient Greeks.

From a practical perspective, this way of war adjudicates "better" and "worse" in terms of maximizing the risk to the enemy and minimizing risk to one's own side. Sociologist Martin Shaw refers to this kind of war as "risk-transfer war," which he sees as synonymous with the Western and American[23] ways of war. In such wars, it will always be preferable to fight in response to threats to national values and interests and in a way that minimizes risk to a society's social, political, and economic institutions. Because of the democratic nature of Western governments, wars must also maximize gain and minimize risk to the political leadership that declared the war. To do so, wars typically must be limited in duration and scope.[24]

In this view, when fighting wars, one must minimize one's own casualties while killing the enemy "efficiently, quickly, and discreetly."[25] Recognizing that war's destruction tends to alienate the electorate and undermine the legitimacy of the war effort, destruction of the enemy is better when it remains "invisible" to the outside world. Such invisibility entails a preference for precision weapons and a reliance on airpower so as to limit risking one's ground forces and inflicting collateral damage. But despite the emphasis on minimizing collateral damage, this way of war will subordinate risk to noncombatants in order to minimize risk to friendly combatants.[26]

It is not hard to see how this view of war shapes its ethics. Just as Clausewitz limits war to military force, the Western ethics of war requires Soldiers to discriminate between targets associated with the enemy's military capability and those that are not. When force protection and mission accomplishment together would seem to put noncombatants at risk, the Western solution is to put force protection at greater risk in favor of reducing noncombatant risk while preserving mission accomplishment. There are limits to this risk. The imperative of mission accomplishment dictates that neither suicide nor mission failure can ever be ethically obligated. Thus Soldiers are not obligated to accept so much risk that they either cannot accomplish the mission or continue the war effort.

Thus, this ethics not only informs the way the United States wages war, but also harmonizes with it. This balance of imperatives does not interfere with the successful waging of war; moreover, by limiting the damage to civilian lives and property, this ethic of war limits post-conflict grievances and facilitates the transition to peace. Of course, there have been times when Western militaries have attacked purely civilian targets. But here is where the exception proves the rule. Even Air Force General Curtis LeMay believed that bombing purely civilian targets was opposed to the law (if not ethics) of war but fell within the scope of how wars are won.[27]

The point of this discussion is not to suggest that the Western way of war is useless. In conventional terms, the U.S. military in particular has often been more effective than its non-Western counterparts. One need not look far for affirmation. The Allied victory over Japan in World War II and the U.S. victory over conventional Iraqi forces in 1991 and 2003 serve as but two examples in a very long list.

But ethics aside, this way of war also has its limitations. The United States defeated the Iraqi military, but it has not yet achieved its political goals in Iraq. Going a little farther back, it is also worth noting that while the U.S. military was successful in its operations against the North Vietnamese military, military success did not achieve the desired political ends. In fact, there have been a number of times when military might actually worked against achieving political ends. The reason is that imposing one's will is only the instrumental end of war. Given that there are other material ends of war, enabled by imposition of will, strategies of attrition and annihilation are not always the best ways to achieve them.

Political scientist Patricia Sullivan attributes such less than optimum approaches to a misalignment between war aims and war strategies. She notes that war aims fall into two broad categories: (1) targets of acceptance, and (2) targets of compliance. The former category involves imposing one's will and thus a certain state of affairs on an enemy. The latter involves pursuading an enemy to see to one's interests and act in a way that realizes and maintains a certain state of affairs. As noted earlier, one succeeds in the former kind of war by pursuing strategies of annihilation and attrition. Sullivan notes, however, that such strategies can often work against targets of compliance. In fact, she notes, when larger states have lost to weaker states in the past, it has often been in attempts to make the weaker state change its policy. This counterintuitive result comes from the fact that while military force can force acceptance, it cannot change someone's mind about what they want.[28] For that, one needs to be able to shape the enemy's interests.

Sun Tzu and the Irregular Way of War.

U.S. adversaries have exploited the misalignment Sullivan has identified. Recognizing that the United States is unrivaled as a conventional military power, these adversaries have largely abandoned the idea that a war with the United States will ever result in imposing their will. Rather, they have undertaken means and ends aimed at compelling the United States to accommodate their interests. To illustrate this point and the implications it has for the U.S. way of war, contrast Clausewitz's view articulated above with that of the ancient Chinese general, Sun Tzu. Noting that war "is a matter of vital importance to the state,"[29] he does not limit its application to the use of military force at all. In fact, he admonishes the would-be general not to put a premium on killing, adding that "to subdue the enemy without fighting is the acme of skill."[30]

Thus, for Sun Tzu, war is paradoxically limited in its goal but unrestricted in its means. But by unrestricted, he is not referring to violence as much as he is the means employed. War begins long before the first shot is fired and requires all the elements of national power to set the conditions for a preferably bloodless acquiescence of the enemy. As historian Michael Handel noted, Sun Tzu "views the political, diplomatic, and logistical preparations for war and the fighting itself as integral parts of the same activity."[31]

Working in the tradition of Sun Tzu, two Chinese senior colonels, Qiao Liang and Wang Xiansui, in the book *Unrestricted Warfare*, argued that failure to recognize this broader view of war is a U.S. vulnerability that weaker states, like China, can exploit.[32] Writing in the aftermath of the 1991 Gulf War, they acknowledged that it would be suicide for any state to take on the U.S. conventional forces. But they also observed that the U.S. military does a poor job of deliberating upon future fights: "lucid and incisive thinking . . . is not a strong point of the Americans. . . . U.S. military preparations for future conflict focus almost exclusively on conventional forces."[33] They go on to point out that "such ridiculous thinking" has caused the United States to be unprepared to fight terrorism and other unconventional threats.[34]

More importantly, the situation they describe would appear to be enduring. This point does not suggest that the United States will never fight a conventional war again. But as long as the United States remains unchallenged in its conventional capabilities, its prudent enemies will avoid directly confronting those capabilities. Employing the language of Clausewitz and Sun Tzu, Qiao and Wang implicitly argue that U.S. conventional success has more or less permanently transformed the character of war: war is no longer "using armed force to compel the enemy to submit to one's will," but rather "using all means, including armed force or nonarmed force, military and nonmilitary, and lethal and nonlethal means to compel the enemy to *accept one's interests*."[35]

Thus, as Dr. Sullivan suggested, the shift of war's aim from imposing one's will to gaining acceptance of one's interests in turn changes what it means to fight well, in both the practical and ethical sense. In this view, military force is just one element of national power that can be used to wage war against an enemy. The list of such elements includes nuclear, diplomatic, financial, network, trade, bio-chemical, intelligence, resources, ecological, psychological, economic aid, space, tactical, regulatory, electronic, smuggling, sanction, guerrilla, drug, news media, terrorist, virtual, ideological warfare, and many more.

Additionally, these elements of warfare can be combined in infinite ways to form various kinds of warfare.[36] For example, the Chinese colonels describe the U.S. war on terror as "national terrorist warfare + intelligence warfare + financial warfare + network warfare + regulatory warfare." They also describe efforts by the Hong Kong government in 1998, just prior to its return to Chinese government control, as a war fought with "financial speculators," using financial warfare combined with regulatory, psychological, and news media "warfare."[37]

From this shift in ends emerges a view of war that expands on Clausewitz, changing war's scope. Friend and enemy are joined by collaborator and competitor;[38] resistance and surrender are replaced by acceptance and rejection; and victory and defeat are replaced by success and failure. Further, friend and enemy do not refer simply to states, but to substate and nonstate organizations as well. Additionally, such conflicts are not zero-sum. If one can achieve one's interests by benefiting the enemy, or some subgroup within the enemy's community, so much the better.

The Ethical Implications of Combating Irregular Threats.

This description of multifaceted warfare against irregular adversaries better accounts for the kinds of conflicts the United States is currently facing. By shifting the emphasis away from imposing one's will to accepting one's interests, this view of war shifts the emphasis of engagement from military capability to the people. This shift subjects civilians and civilian institutions to competing efforts of co-option and coercion where both sides attempt either to win the populace to its cause or prevent the enemy from doing the same. As Rupert Smith notes in *The Utility of Force*, in such conflicts, the loyalties, attitudes, and quality of life of the people do not simply impact the outcome of a conflict: they determine it.[39] Because of this shift in emphasis, Smith argues that these conflicts are best described as "wars amongst the peoples" where the enemy operates among the civilian population in part because of one's conventional prohibitions against targeting them.[40]

Operating within the civilian population, the enemy depends on that population for shelter, food, medical assistance, finances, and other types of support. This relationship entails collaboration on the part of some, if not all, of that population, though it does not follow that this support is given willingly: the ability of the enemy to exact it determines his strength. Hamas, for example, routinely places rocket and mortar positions near schools, residences, and other civilian sites to exploit any resulting collateral damage. Similarly, it forcibly moves civilians into areas where the Israelis are expected to attack.[41]

Willing or not, this relationship draws the civilian population into a status logically inseparable from warfighting, making them necessary, if not legitimate, targets of war. What makes them necessary targets is the fact that the irregulars (or militarily weaker side) could not fight without their support, and we (the militarily stronger side) cannot win if we do not undermine it.

The Ethics of Combating Irregular Adversaries.

This shift in emphasis from combat forces to populations poses a significant ethical as well as practical challenge to the Western way of war. In terms of practical challenges, population emphasis suggests that the United States must incorporate all the elements of national power to ensure success; moreover, to realize its interests, it must do so in a way that both coerces and attracts the population. It is beyond the scope of this discussion to amplify this point much further. But it does suggest that there is an ethical as well as practical requirement to develop and implement these broader means. In ethical terms, the challenge arises because of the intermingling of combatant and noncombatant as adversaries exploit civilian populations. Challenges also result, of course, from the necessaary prohibitions intended to protect the population from the suffering caused by war.

It is for this reason that combating irregular threats does not lend itself to the easy dichotomies of civilian-military or combatant-noncombatant. Irregular actors hide among civilian populations, making civilians complicit, if not willingly so, in their activities. But one must not assume that civilian complicity and liability cause a loss of their immunity when we operate against irregular threats. This line of argument is essentially the same as the one made by controversial academic Ward Churchill in echoing Osama Bin Laden's justification for striking the World Trade Center in New York. Alleging the Twin Towers occupants' indirect contribution to American military might, both argued that the terrorist attacks of September 11, 2001, were justified because of their relationship to U.S. military policies they believed were unjust. Setting aside the sheer illogic of these claims, it is worth examining whether and to what extent civilians should be targeted in the course of combating irregular threats.[42]

Thus, it does not follow that by virtue of being members of a particular population, individuals have necessarily made a choice that justifies our killing or even targeting them. However, to the extent that a government or other political entity represents itself as a threat to some other group, the way its members choose to participate in that effort can affect whether or to what degree they may be ethically exposed to certain kinds of retaliation. As the philosopher Thomas Nagel notes, a person may be subjected to hostile treatment by virtue of the threat that person represents, since "hostility or aggression should be directed at its true object."[43]

In Nagel's view, one is ethically permitted to subject a person to hostile treatment only because of something that person does, and further, the hostile treatment must be directed at the person in virtue of the threat posed. In conventional *jus in bello* terms, it follows from this argument that combatants may be killed, since they embody the threat represented by the enemy state; and noncombatants may not, since by virtue of being noncombatants, they do not represent that threat. Of course, this argument does not necessarily exempt civilians from being targeted. For example, it is permissible to target munitions workers even though they are not uniformed members of the military. This permission is due to the fact that their activity is not logically inseparable from warfighting.[44]

Discrimination: Enemies, Criminals, and a Just Peace.

In determining what measures are permissible in such a complex environment, one must also take into account the ethical aim of the state's use of force in the first place. Despite the change in the character of war, the fundamental question about the ethicality of war is still a question of justice. While there are many concepts and forms of justice, at its most basic justice is about getting what one deserves.[45] In the context of national security, what one deserves is what one has a right to, which as I have previously stipulated is, at a minimum, life and liberty.

The responsibility for ensuring that individuals enjoy such rights falls on the state by virtue of the social contract. The state ensures these rights by creating law enforcement and military institutions that provide the kind of security required for the exercise of those rights. Security, being indivisible and nonexcludable, is a public good, meaning that its provision is subject to the demands of distributive justice.[46]

Providing security requires the sovereign to form institutions around which the distribution of social goods is organized. These institutions identify a public system of rules that define how other individuals, which I will refer to as the state's agents, identify their positions, rights, roles, and duties.[47] Institutions, in this sense, can be both abstract and concrete. For example, one may speak of "the military" when determining the roles, rights, duties, powers, prohibitions, permissions, and obligations associated with certain aspects of national security.[48] More concretely, one may refer to the "Department of the Defense (DoD)," which is the practical U.S. manifestation of "the military" actually charged with the roles and responsibilities associated with maintaining national security. Collectively, the institutions which employ the various powers of the state *are* the state. Individuals who operate within these institutions thus take on the obligations of the state insofar as the exercise of such obligations is compatible with the role they play within that institution.

It is important to note, however, that despite the fact that military and law enforcement institutions share a common purpose—to protect citizens of their state—they differ significantly because of the different kinds of threats they confront. Militaries confront enemies who are capable of violating the state's right to political sovereignty and territorial integrity. Criminals, on the other hand, threaten individual rights. While widespread criminal activity can place so much pressure on government institutions that they collapse, normally they do not represent a threat to the state itself. How these dual roles inform the ethics of combating irregular threats is discussed later.

It is, of course, beyond the scope of this paper to establish what appropriate state institutions should exist, given the range of cultural, social, and political conditions. But the paper does suggest that if the purpose of fighting wars is to establish a just peace, then, once established, the purpose of continued military operations is to maintain that peace. A just peace entails not simply a cessation of hostilities, but the presence of just institutions capable of sustaining that peace. Given these considerations, one can say a state of peace exists under the following conditions: [49]

- The enemy is defeated or transformed into a nonexistential threat either to one's state or to the imposition of a just host-nation government.

- There exist institutions necessary for enforcing the rule of law, including police, courts, and prisons.
- These institutions must be fair, honest, and credible, where citizens are willing to rely on them to resolve disputes rather than resort to violence to resolve disputes themselves.

Of course, these conditions do not spontaneously emerge when the war ends. In fact, it may not be clear when a particular conflict ends. There is no clear signal, like an offer of surrender, marking when an irregular threat no longer exists. If the enemy does surrender, it usually comes long after the threat has been contained. As a matter of course, "winning" is usually manifested by the ability of one side to impose its order on the population in question, however that population is identified.

This point means that counterinsurgent forces must often transition from conditions of war, where no institutions associated with civil society exist, to conditions of peace where such institutions come into existence and are capable of enforcing the just rule of law on their own. It is a fact of many conflict and post-conflict situations that even when such institutions exist, they are not always effective. Institutional development in conflict and post-conflict situations proceeds in stages. It begins with imposing order, then transitions to protecting minority rights, and then ends with local institutions capable of sustaining a just social order.[50]

As the operating environment transitions from warfighting to civil society, the state's obligation to protect its citizens may fall on foreign military forces supporting it as well. Whatever the actual reasons the higher headquarters had in the ROE contretemps discussed earlier, it was right to take into account how the sergeant's request for smoke and illumination might endanger civilians. As the Afghan government continues to develop institutions necessary to provide security in a just manner, U.S. forces must not only shoulder their responsibility to avoid harm to themselves, but also their responsibility to protect those civilians. Figure 2 depicts the inverse relationship between the strength of civil institutions on one hand, and permissions regarding the use of force and collateral damage on the other. As the capability of civil institutions increases to the point that they are strong enough to provide basic security needs for a given population, collateral damage becomes no longer permissible since it represents the kind of violence those institutions are supposed to prevent.

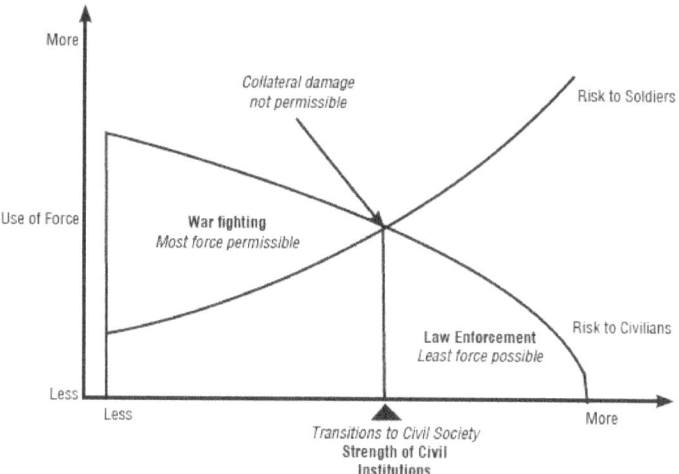

Figure 2. The Inverse Relationship between the Strength of Civil Institutions and Permissions Regarding the Use of Force and Collateral Damage.

Thus, as civil institutions become stronger, susceptibility to risk decreases for civilians while increasing for Soldiers, as well as police and other security services. In other words, the risk shifts from civilian to security provider.

Whether the decision to withhold fire support was in fact the right one depends on whether the state, in fact, had control over that territory. As noted earlier, the state's responsibility to protect is enabled by its right to sovereignty and territory. Where an enemy has effectively taken territory and displaced the state's institutions, then the threat is no longer criminal, and great force is permitted. This point will be discussed in more detail later.

However, as this example shows, in the context of this transition from war to peace, the central difficulty when combating irregular threats is sorting out the combatants from enemy collaborators among one's own supporters. This sorting is further complicated by the fact that some collaborators are coerced, and some nominal allies have ties to and even sympathies for the enemy. Additional complications arise when, unlike in conventional conflicts, the activities of insurgents and their supporters take place in the same space as routine and peaceful civilian activity, making it difficult to determine who is complicit with the enemy and who is not.

Thus as a practical matter, distinguishing between combatant, noncombatant, and supported can be very difficult, if not impossible. In such contexts, restricting one's efforts to engaging only armed elements of the insurgency can have the dual effect of jeopardizing the stronger side's chances for victory, and prolonging the conflict, paradoxically leading to more harm to noncombatants.

Resolving the paradox requires expanding the set of legitimate targets while reducing the occasions for the lethal use of force. Further, in expanding the set of legitimate targets, one must take into account their relationship to the actual threat Soldiers face. Taken together, these points suggest the following permissions and restrictions regarding the requirement to discriminate permissible targets from the impermissibles:

- Members of the general population may be subject to law enforcement measures regardless of their level of cooperation with the enemy, such as curfews and increased security measures, as well as information operations.
- Members of the population who indirectly, but unknowingly, support enemy activities may be required to cease such activities, even if it negatively impacts their quality of life.
- Members of the population who directly and knowingly support the enemy but do not engage in violent activities—the actual threat they represent being indirect and they being no threat if there were no enemy—may not be targeted for killing, but rather must be treated as criminals.
- Members of the population who participate in violent activities may be killed or detained. To the extent that these members of the population represent a threat to the government, collateral damage may be permitted.
- Members of insurgent and terrorist groups may be targeted for killing if they represent an enemy threat in the sense described above. If they represent a criminal threat, again in the

sense described above, they must be targeted as criminals and killed only when it is not possible to detain them.

In addition to standard *jus in bello* restraints, this analysis also suggests that it would not be permissible to target the following:

- Members of the population who, if targeted, will not have an effect on the outcome of the conflict. This is not controversial, as no theory of just war would endorse gratuitous targeting.
- Members of the general population may not be harmed, even collaterally, if the threat represented by the adversary may best be described as criminal.

SUMMING UP: BALANCING COMPETING IMPERATIVES

As discussed above, the aim of operations against irregular adversaries should be the establishment of a just civil society capable of securing the rights of its members without representing a threat to the rights of members of other societies. As in Iraq and Afghanistan, such conflicts often start as wars, where combatants are relatively easy to distinguish from noncombatants. In such cases, traditional just war norms would apply.

However, as these conflicts also show, the battlefield defeat of those forces does not always mean an end to fighting. However, though the fighting continues, it does not follow that the conflict is unchanged. Where the major combat operations that began the war were aimed at imposing U.S. will on the Iraqi and Taliban governments, after their defeat the aim of the war transitioned to persuading elements of the population to accept the other's interest and manifest that acceptance in the form of a government they would all accept.

What norms apply then depends on the kind of threat the adversary represents. At this point, war-fighting ceases to be about defeating enemy forces but compelling the population to accept the legitimacy of a new government. The burden of risk thereupon should shift to reflect the rights and responsibilities of that government. If the rights of a state rest on its citizens' rights to life and liberty, individuals and groups that threaten those individual rights but not the state's rights, are then best conceived as criminal. While they do not directly threaten those state's rights, their threat to individual rights still places a burden on the new state to protect those individual rights.

When it comes to the use of force, military and law enforcement organizations instruct their forces to always use the least force necessary. However, these entities have very different conceptions regarding what is the least force necessary. Under conventional just war norms, the military seeks to use the most force permissible, given the requirements of proportionality and discrimination. In the conditions of civil society, law enforcement seeks to use the least force possible. The different conceptions are due to the way each perceives and is trained to deal with threats. To the police, the threat is a criminal they must apprehend in order to minimize disruption to society. Since the use of violence represents a further disruption of the peace, police are always looking to use the least force possible. In this view, no use of force where civilian bystanders will knowingly, though unintentionally, be harmed is permitted.

However, Soldiers are trained to defeat enemies who must be killed if there is to be peace. They are always looking to reduce risk to themselves by using the most force they have available. As noted previously, that force should be tempered by the amount of risk Soldiers must assume rather than putting noncombatants at risk.[51] This feature of conflict gives us two models of threat that states may face: warfighting and law enforcement. States have developed different institutions to deal with each; they employ very different forces, methods, and ethics in facing those threats. These divergent conceptions of necessity determine different permissions regarding the use of force.

Mission Accomplishment and Proportionality.

In both models, mission accomplishment remains an imperative. Typically, Soldiers may risk only mission failure — or more accurately, forgo the mission altogether — when the degree of risk assigned to noncombatants results in harm done that is disproportionate to the good achieved.[52] When calculating proportionality, Soldiers fighting enemies must weigh the harm the Soldiers do against the requirements of future peace. Actions that will perpetuate animosity and make a stable peace difficult to attain need to be weighed against any action intended to achieve that peace. Soldiers engaging criminals are obligated to weigh the harm done against the requirements of the current peace. This restriction would not only limit engaging in violent actions, it would also preclude nonviolent actions that nonetheless disrupted the peace, such as mass detentions or excessive restrictions on movement.

Force Protection.

As noted above, the degree of risk Soldiers are obligated to accept is limited only by the requirements of force protection and mission accomplishment. Under the law enforcement model, Soldiers are obligated to accept certain risks so as to prevent harm to civilians, but they may not put those civilians at risk.[53] There are conditions, for example, in which law enforcement officials will allow a suspect to escape rather than put bystanders at risk of serious physical injury or death. However, they would not stop their pursuit of that criminal nor their efforts to prevent future criminal acts.[54] Thus, if the choice is to forgo harming civilians or conducting a particular mission, Soldiers must choose to forgo conducting that mission. This requirement does not mean, however, they must forgo achieving their objective, just that they must find another way to do it. Additionally, like police, Soldiers are not obligated to risk serious physical harm or death simply to apprehend a single individual unless that individual represents an immediate harm to others.

Minimizing Harm.

When discriminating between legitimate and illegitimate targets, Soldiers fighting enemies must observe the negative obligation to minimize noncombatant casualties. Soldiers engaging criminals must avoid such casualties altogether. Additionally, under the criminal model, Soldiers have a positive obligation to protect civilians from harm in the same way police have an obligation to protect civilians.[55] This latter condition assumes that Soldiers can act as police in the given area of operations. Where that authority does not exist, Soldiers may engage the adversary under the enemy model, but only in order to establish a law enforcement capability as rapidly as possible.[56]

IMPLICATIONS FOR LEADERS

What should be obvious from this framework is that the identity of the military professional will have to evolve to meet the demands of the environment of operating against irregular adversaries. The good qualities of an officer derive from the purpose and function of the profession and the environment in which it is practiced.[57] As the function and the environment change, so must the defining qualities of the good officer.

When fighting enemies, qualities such as decisiveness, aggressiveness, and unwillingness to compromise are essential to achieving peace. Under the criminal model, traits such as tact, restraint, diplomacy, and patience are paramount. Balancing the requirements of these sometimes competing models poses a problem for the officer. In fact, several studies have noted that the "professional career Soldier is not necessarily the best person for peace-keeping (or law enforcement) tasks."[58]

It is worth noting that the traits described above for both models are not necessarily mutually exclusive. The difference derives from which traits dominate. Thus the challenge for the officer is to cultivate new traits, while not allowing the old ones to atrophy. Additionally, the officer will have to develop the judgment to determine how these traits apply across a range of environments.[59]

As previously discussed, combating irregular threats requires Soldiers to have a great deal of local knowledge so they may best account for local needs and interests in order to bolster the supported state. However, the higher one is in the chain of command, the more difficult it is to retain and apply this knowledge in the context of a particular operation. This feature of irregular warfighting puts pressure on traditional Army culture, which assigns near total responsibility to the commander for whatever happens in his or her command. As a result, commanders tend to retain at their level the authority to make critical decisions, a tendency resulting in relatively centralized decisionmaking.

However, as the sergeant in the ROE example experienced, while higher headquarters are adept at applying general rules and guidance, they cannot—at least not consistently and effectively—take into account the many nuances associated with combating irregular threats, such as the relative value of any particular operation, the relationship of particular locals to enemy forces, or how much risk civilians will be exposed to by a particular course of action. As a result, what emerges is a cacophony of decisions that sometimes place Soldiers at extreme risk and at other times lead to unnecessary civilian casualties.

It is beyond the scope of this discussion to fully articulate the implications of this point for traditional command responsibility, but it does follow that decisions regarding the use of force should be made at the lowest level feasible. This will require leaders to have extremely good local knowledge, since they will have to live with both the negative and positive consequences of their decisions. However, a leader who has developed a sense of obligation toward members of the local population will be in a better position to determine what level of force is appropriate within the framework articulated in this discussion.

IMPLICATIONS FOR THE PROFESSION

This monograph suggests the following measures the profession should take to provide the officer corps with the wherewithal necessary to conduct ethical operations when facing irregular adversaries:

- Develop the capability to conduct law enforcement operations and establish civil institutions in post-conflict environments. Application of force under the criminal model depends on access to functioning law enforcement institutions. These institutions are usually not available to foreign forces. This suggests that when confronting irregular adversaries, militaries must incorporate this institutional capability into their organization. In some cases, this capability development will require integrating military and civilian capabilities under a unified command. Failing to invest in such capabilities will lead to increased risk to noncombatants that could have been reasonably avoided. To the extent that a supporting state would have invested in those capabilities to avoid risk to its own citizens in similar circumstances, it should do so as well when conducting operations in foreign countries.

- In environments where the enemy is sufficiently strong to prevent the establishment of such institutions, Soldiers may conduct operations under the enemy model even though the adversary may not meet the enemy criteria. But these operations must include the goal of creating an environment where police methods and forces would be effective.

- Modify ROE to reflect the restrictions inherent in the criminal model. Additionally, commanders will need to develop a framework for shifting between the two models.
- Increase the use of and training in nonlethal weapons. This will give Soldiers more options when dealing with situations where it is difficult to discriminate between combatants and noncombatants.
- Revise the ethical development of officers to include traits associated with law enforcement and peacekeeping, while preserving those normally associated with warfighting.
- Revise the conception of command responsibility and intra-command risk-sharing to permit greater decentralization regarding the decision to use force. Place the decision to use force at the lowest level feasible. Determining the appropriate level should take into account the individual leader's experience and knowledge of the local environment as well as the means employed in achieving military objectives.

CONCLUSION

If one views the character of war as the imposition of one's will on the enemy, then one will naturally emphasize coercive strategies of attrition and annihilation that eliminate resistance. Such a view, of course, does not ignore constraints in war, but as the distinction between what is and is not logically separable from warfighting blurs, the range of potential targets expands. As it does, the burden of risk shifts to the civilian population, increasing the potential for human rights violations.

On the other hand, if one's view of war favors compelling the enemy to accept one's interests, then one must employ a mix of coercive and persuasive inducements aimed at shaping the enemy's interests in conforming. While this view does not ignore the requirement to kill, it often subordinates eliminating enemy combat capabilities in favor of achieving complementary political goals. As the distinction between politics and warfighting blurs, risk shifts back to combatants, who must often sacrifice short-term military goals for the sake of long-term institutional development. But if one over-emphasizes such attractive measures over coercive ones, one creates space for the enemy to operate, prolonging the war and putting one's own Soldiers — as well as civilians — at unnecessary risk.

Placing the burden of risk on the enemy means placing it on the civilian population as well. One could, and in some cases should, accept more risk to one's citizens and Soldiers, but if one treats that imperative as an absolute, one abandons one's obligation to those persons as well. In these kinds of conflicts, it is not uncommon to feel that one is placed in the position not of balancing ethical demands, but of abandoning them.

However, abandoning one's ethical obligations is not only unethical, it is unnecessary. It is, of course, beyond our scope here to fully spell out how one should balance these imperatives in each instance. However, what this analysis has shown is that when combating irregular threats in environments where stable peace exists, Soldiers are ethically obligated to employ means that avoid harm to noncombatants. In environments where there is no peace, Soldiers may undertake actions that place noncombatants at risk, but must observe the traditional restrictions of proportionality and discrimination.

The fact that enemy and criminal threats are often found within the same battle space provides extraordinary ethical as well as practical challenges to officers of all ranks. To confront such threats without betraying the rights and values Soldiers are defending, military leaders must reconsider the application of force. This will require not only radical adjustments to training, force development, and task organization, it will also require a fundamental rethinking of the Soldier's identity.

ENDNOTES

1. While the observation of these restrictions has certainly been inconsistent across multiple conflicts, nonetheless, for the most part militaries recognize these restrictions and have avoided employing weapons and tactics that are inherently indiscriminate.

2. U.S. Training and Doctrine Command (TRADOC) *Pamphlet (Pam) 525-3-0, The Army Capstone Concept, Operational Adaptability: Operating under Conditions of Uncertainty and Complexity in an Era of Persistent Conflict*, 2016-2028, Washington, DC: Department of the Army, December 21, 2009. Finding the right label for the kind of unconventional conflicts discussed in this monograph is difficult, as the literature is rarely consistent. As the Army Capstone concept defines it, irregular warfare is the "violent struggle among state and non-state actors for legitimacy and influence over the relevant population(s)." However, this term risks arbitrarily excluding operations against irregular adversaries that fall short of war. "Asymmetric warfare," which is an arguably more popular term, still raises objections from a number of authors and scholars who are concerned that it does not sufficiently distinguish between conventional asymmetries, where one side simply brings more firepower to the field than the other from the range of 21st century security threats, which use unexpected means to strike at vulnerable points. Rupert Smith, author of *Utility of Force*, for example, views the term as simplistic and prefers "war amongst the peoples." T. X. Hammes, author of *The Sling and the Stone*, argues that wars characterized by the use of asymmetric means such as terrorism and insurgency are best described as *fourth gen-*

eration war, where first generation warfare focused on destroying the enemy's "close" forces, second generation warfare employed firepower to destroy enemy forces in range, and third generation warfare employed maneuver to strike at enemy command and control as well as logistic capabilities. Fourth generation warfare changes the focus of war from the enemy's military capability to the will of the people. For the purposes of this discussion, I will distinguish between "regular war" and combating "irregular threats."

3. George Will, "U.S. tactics in Afghanistan put troops at risk," *The Washington Post,* June 21, 2010, available from *www.courant.com/ news/opinion/hc-will-afghanistan-tactics-0621-20100621,0,2660470. column.*

4. Dexter Filkins, "The Fall of the Warrior King," *New York Times Magazine*, October 23, 2005, p. 54.

5. *Ibid.*, p. 57.

6. "Karzai Demands Halt to Civilian Casualties," *Reuters,* February 7, 2010, available from *www.rferl.org/content/Karzai_ Demands_Halt_To_Afghan_Civilian_Casualties/1951260.html.*

7. A. Karzai, "Lament; Afghanistan's president becomes a NATO scold," *The Wall Street Journal (Online)*, February 24, 2010, available from *www.proquest.com/.*

8. Michael Walzer, *Just and Unjust Wars*, 2nd Ed., New York: Basic Books, 1992, pp. 130-132. According to Walzer, all a utilitarian ethic can do is either confirm our intuitions regarding the rules of war or suggest they be overridden, as under utility theory, no act is immoral by virtue of its character, only its outcome. Walzer does argue that cases of "supreme emergencies," where the realization of catastrophic harm is imminent, may justify the use of means normally ethically off-limits.

9. All theories of utility emphasize the maximization of some good and the minimization of some harm. They disagree, however, on what exactly the good is. For the father of utility theory, Jeremy Bentham, it was pleasure. For John Stuart Mill, it was happiness. Others consider it interest or well-being. In the context of

Just War thinking, the good is understood as victory for the just side, which is the best outcome of any war, even for the enemy. See William Shaw, "The Consequentialist Perspective," James Dreier, ed., *Contemporary Debates in Moral Theory*, Malden, MA: Blackwell Publishing, 2006, p. 10.

10. Proportionality is a notoriously difficult requirement to calculate as it requires one to measure harms that are not always commensurate, as well as calculate the future harms one is trying to avoid. Thus, when considering the Israeli case, one must consider the impact Hamas attacks over the last several years has had on the quality of life of the affected Israeli towns. The fact the attacks were not particularly effective did not mean that those living in those villages were less terrorized. Now calculating how much collateral damage on the Palestinian side is proportional to the objective of preventing future attacks and restoring a sense of normalcy to the affected Israeli villages is difficult, but not impossible, to determine. Additionally, one must calculate the harms expected from future attacks, which requires one to consider second and third order consequences as well. For example, if Israel failed to prevent the attacks, Hamas may be emboldened to increase them. In both cases, judgments are difficult, but not impossible. It is beyond the scope of this monograph to examine fully the complexities associated with calculating proportionality, but what should be clear is that proportionality must be measured in terms of the overall good achieved by attaining the military objective, not the current "balance of harm" each side has endured.

11. Because the immediate, short-term military objectives are embedded in the larger, overall military objective, proportionality calculations apply to both. But when it comes to the more limited, short-term objectives, proportionality must be calculated in terms of its contribution to that objective, not in terms of the value of the overall objective.

12. I will use the term "Soldier" to refer generically to uniformed members of the military. I will capitalize "Soldier," "Sailor," and "Airman" when referring to uniformed members of the Army, Navy, and Air Force just as one would capitalize "Marine" when referring to uniformed members of the U.S. Marine Corps.

13. James M. Dubik, "Human Rights, Command Responsibility, and Walzer's Just War Theory," *Philosophy and Public Affairs,* Vol. 11, No. 4, 1982, p. 355. Dubik rejects Walzer's conception that Soldiers give up their right to life to gain the right to kill. He argues that if rights to life and liberty are indeed natural, then Soldiers — or anyone for that matter — cannot give them up.

14. Walzer, pp. 53-54.

15. Paul Christopher, *The Ethics of War and Peace: An Introduction to Legal and Moral Issues,* 2nd Ed., Trenton, NJ: Prentice Hall, 1999, pp. 164-166. It does follow from this analysis that states that threaten the lives and liberty of their citizens do not enjoy the rights of political sovereignty and territorial integrity. This rationale has been used to justify humanitarian interventions, such as those in Bosnia and Kosovo. See Walzer, pp. 101-108.

16. Walzer, pp. 151-152.

17. Dubik.

18. Obviously, these actions are immoral from the perspective of the Just War Tradition, and are war crimes from the perspective of international law. By fighting in an immoral and illegal manner, groups like Hamas expose themselves to justified reprisals, which would permit the Israeli Defense Force to engage in otherwise immoral activity to dissuade Hamas from continued crimes. However, reprisals may be directed only at those responsible for the crime in first place, which would preclude targeting noncombatant lives and property. See Walzer, pp. 207-216.

19. Christopher, p. 93.

20. Peter Paret, "Education, Politics, and War in the Life of Clausewitz," *Journal of the History of Ideas,* Vol. 29, No. 3, Jul-Sep, 1968, p. 395. That Clausewitz would express himself this way is not surprising, given his exposure to philosophers like Kant, who emphasized the role of will, and Friedrich Hegel, who emphasized a dialectical process of reasoning. But Paret notes that while Clausewitz was certainly exposed to Hegel and Kant, he did not seem to apply their insights directly to his own views of politics and war. Thus one must be careful when inferring philosophical

influences on his writing. But while it seems clear that Clause-witz did not deliberately employ a Hegelian dialectic to construct a full-blown philosophy, I am suggesting he was influenced by the methods of great thinkers like Kant and Hegel in how he approached the subject.

21. Victor D. Hanson, *Carnage and Culture: Landmark Battles in the Rise of Western Power*, New York: Doubleday, Random House, Inc., 2001, p. 22.

22. *Ibid.*, p. 21.

23. For the purposes of this discussion, I will refer to the way of war that emerges from the kind of thinking I have associated with Clausewitz as the "Western Way of War," which I take to be roughly synonymous to the American way of war. Although, as a matter of practice it may be more accurate to say there are many American ways of war of which the irregular way of war that will be articulated in this discussion may eventually be one.

24. Martin Shaw, *The New Western Way of War,* Cambridge, UK: Polity Press, 2005, pp. 71-78.

25. *Ibid.*, pp. 79-97.

26. *Ibid.*, p. 97.

27. In the full context of his remarks, General LeMay argued that war is itself immoral, implying that restrictions on the use of force that prolonged it were also immoral. Thus, while recognizing the illegality of the bombings, it is also fairly clear he did believe these actions were immoral.

28. Patricia L. Sullivan, "War Aims and War Outcomes: Why Powerful States Lose Limited Wars," *Journal of Conflict Resolution,* Vol. 51. No. 5, June 2007, p. 505.

29. Sun Tzu, *The Art of War,* Samuel B. Griffith, ed., Oxford, UK: Oxford University Press, 1971, p. 63.

30. *Ibid.*, p. 77.

31. Michael I. Handel, *Masters of War: Classical Strategic Thought,* 3rd Ed., Portland, OR: Frank Cass Publishers, 2001, p. 27.

32. Qiao Liang and Wang Xiangsui, *Unrestricted Warfare,* Beijing, China: PLA Literature and Arts Publishing House, February 1999, English translation available from *www.terrorism.com/documents/TRC-Analysis/unrestricted.pdf* .

33. *Ibid.,* p. 24.

34. *Ibid.,* p. 145.

35. *Ibid.,* p. 7 (italics by author). In fact, as Qiao and Wang note, "(t)o a very great extent, war is no longer even war but rather coming to grips on the internet, and matching the mass media, assault and defense . . . along with other things which we had never viewed as war," p. 140.

36. *Ibid.,* p. 146.

37. *Ibid.,* p. 147. This thinking is reflected more comprehensively in the People's Liberation Army's (PLA) concept of *shashoujian* or "Assassin's Mace." Assassin's Mace is an umbrella term for doctrinal development and acquisition of weapons systems aimed at enabling the "inferior" to defeat the "superior." This doctrine relies on surprise as well as deceptive and unorthodox methods "unknown to the adversary." The means employed under this doctrine—such as those described above—are intended to achieve the effects of deterrence, decapitation, blinding, paralyzing, or disintegrating enemy forces. Jason E. Bruzdzinsi, "Demystifying Shashoulian: China's "Assassin's Mace Concept," Andrew Scobell and Larry Wortzel, eds., *Civil Military Change in China: Elites, Institutes, and Ideas After the 16th Party Congress,* Carlisle, PA: Strategic Studies Institute, U.S. Army War College, 2004.

38. I use the term "collaborator" to define those persons who offer some sort of cooperation with the enemy, whether they do so willingly or not.

39. Rupert Smith, *The Utility of Force: The Art of War in the Modern World,* New York: Alfred A. Knopf, 2007, p. 281.

40. *Ibid.*, pp. 19-20.

41. Human Rights Watch, *Rockets from Gaza,* August 6, 2009, available from *www.hrw.org/en/node/8567/section/1.*

42. Ward Churchill, "Some People Push Back: On the Justice of Roosting Chickens,"available from *www.kersplebedeb.com/ mystuff/s11/churchill.html.* See also "Chickening out," *The Village Voice*, February 23, 2005, available from *www.proquest.com/.*

43. Thomas Nagel, "War and Massacre," originally published in *Philosophy and Public Affairs,* Vol. 1, 1972, pp. 123-144. Reprinted in Gregory Reichberg, Henrik Syse, and Endre Begby eds., *The Ethics of War*, Oxford, UK: Blackwell Publishing, 2006, pp. 654-656.

44. *Ibid.*, p. 656.

45. Robert Audi, ed., *The Cambridge Dictionary of Philosophy,* Cambridge, UK: Cambridge University Press, 1995, p. 395.

46. Michael Taylor, *The Possibility of Cooperation*, Cambridge, UK: Cambridge University Press, 1995, p. 5.

47. John Rawls, *A Theory of Justice*, Cambridge, MA: Belknap Press, 1971, p. 35.

48. *Ibid.*, p. 55.

49. These conditions are adapted from Tony Pfaff, "Military Ethics in Complex Contingencies," Don Snider and Lloyd Matthews, eds., *Transformation of the Army Profession,* 2nd Ed., Boston, MA: McGraw Hill, 2005, p. 413.

50. Michael J. Dziedzic and Leonard Hawley, *The Quest for a Viable Peace*, Washington, DC: United States Institute of Peace, 2009, p. 17.

51. Tony Pfaff, "Military Ethics in Complex Contingencies," Don M. Snider and Lloyd J. Matthews, eds., *The Future of the Army Profession,* 2nd Ed., New York: McGraw Hill, 2005, pp. 412-414.

52. There may also be cases where Soldiers may be morally permitted to forgo missions if they face certain death. Intuitively, however, this idea generally runs counter to the obligation of the Soldier to defend the state and its citizens. Resolving such conflicts is difficult since they may entail circumstances where Soldiers are obligated to risk death. It is beyond the scope of this discussion, however, to go into those concerns in detail.

53. For example, New York City Police Department policy prohibits the use of deadly force when doing so will endanger innocent persons. This policy also prohibits police officers from discharging their firearms to subdue a fleeing felon as long as that felon does not represent an *immediate* (author's italics) threat of death or serious physical injury to themselves or others. Email from New York City Police Inspector Michael Hurley, April 22, 2010.

54. In most U.S. jurisdictions, police would be prohibited from attempting to kill a violent criminal if bystanders would certainly be harmed. This is true regardless of how many others the police officer may think may be harmed by the criminal's escape. See John Kleinig, Chap. 1, *The Ethics of Policing,* Cambridge, MA: Cambridge University Press, 1996.

55. Paolo Tripoldi, "Peacekeepers, Moral Autonomy, and the Use of Force," *Journal of Military Ethics*, Vol. 5, No. 3, 2006, p. 217.

56. Such permission is a concession to the fact that terrorist groups like Hamas do not neatly fall into either category. Otherwise, the state would be in the paradoxical position of having to fail in its duty to protect its citizens in order to uphold the rights of a population, elements of which threaten those citizens, simply because it cannot conduct law enforcement operations in that territory. This seems unreasonable. It seems equally unreasonable, however, to suggest that simply because a terrorist group operates outside the reach of a states' police forces that the open-ended use of military force is permitted. Otherwise, any state could rationalize the use of military force against any state where terrorists are conducting operations. Thus such use must be clearly directed at creating the conditions for law enforcement operations—whether conducted by the threatened state or host nation police forces where the terrorists are operating. This, in fact, has been a feature

of U.S. operations in Iraq and Afghanistan, where military force is often employed to prevent local police forces from being overwhelmed or co-opted by insurgents.

57. Charles A. (Tony) Pfaff, "Officership: Character, Leadership, and Ethical Decision Making," *Military Review,* March-April, 2003, p. 68.

58. Tripoldi, p. 217.

59. Pfaff, "Officership," pp. 70-71. The author addresses an outline for officer character development.

www.ingramcontent.com/pod-product-compliance
Lightning Source LLC
Chambersburg PA
CBHW060008300526
45794CB00003B/1132